THIS COUPON ENTITLES YOU TO

ORAL **BLINDFOLD**

Wear a blindfold while I slowly kiss my way down between your legs

THIS COUPON ENTITLES YOU TO

HEAVY **PETTING**

20 minute hot foreplay session in a location of your choice
(restrain from having full sex to intensify the sexual tension)

I want to get

HOT & HEAVY

with you

I want to get

HOT & HEAVY

with you

THIS COUPON ENTITLES YOU TO

ONE LICK **IT OFF SESSION**

I'll cover your body with something sweet and sticky then slowly lick it off

THIS COUPON ENTITLES YOU TO

FULL **BODY MASSAGE**

45 minute intimate massage covering EVERY inch of your hot body

I want to get

HOT & HEAVY

with you

I want to get

HOT & HEAVY

with you

THIS COUPON ENTITLES YOU TO

SEXUAL **FANTASY PLAY**

One of your wettest, dirtiest dreams brought to life

THIS COUPON ENTITLES YOU TO

A STRIP **TEASE**

20 minute private lap dance finishing with a full striptease
(no touching the dancer during the act please)

I want to get

HOT & HEAVY

with you

I want to get

HOT & HEAVY

with you

THIS COUPON ENTITLES YOU TO

A KITCHEN **QUICKIE**

Against the sink, over the counter, on top of the washing machine - you decide
(must not last longer than six minutes and must be fully clothed - side pantie style)

THIS COUPON ENTITLES YOU TO

NO **HANDS**

Up to 20 minutes of caressing and teasing your body with my lips, tongue,
breath, skin… anything EXCEPT my hands

I want to get

HOT & HEAVY

with you

I want to get

HOT & HEAVY

with you

THIS COUPON ENTITLES YOU TO

ONE HOTEL **HOOKUP**

Let's get dressed up and pretend we're strangers who meet at a bar
then proceed to having a sordid one night stand in a cheap hotel

THIS COUPON ENTITLES YOU TO

FRUITY **LUBES**

Let's experiment with as many fruity flavored lubes as we can handle

I want to get

HOT & HEAVY

with you

I want to get

HOT & HEAVY

with you

THIS COUPON ENTITLES YOU TO

A SEX **MARATHON SESSION**

Sex all night long (or until we're too exhausted to continue)

THIS COUPON ENTITLES YOU TO

EROTIC **RE-ENACTMENT**

That hot scene from a sexy movie you've enjoyed... let's do it

I want to get

HOT & HEAVY

with you

I want to get

HOT & HEAVY

with you

THIS COUPON ENTITLES YOU TO

EXPERIMENTAL **PLAY**

Experiment with sex toys or food items of your choosing

THIS COUPON ENTITLES YOU TO

MORNING **SEX**

Midweek quickie before work, or slow and sleepy weekender - your choice

I want to get

HOT & HEAVY

with you

I want to get

HOT & HEAVY

with you

THIS COUPON ENTITLES YOU TO

NAKED **BUTT-LER**

I'll prepare your meal with nothing on except a bow tie and a smile
(includes meal prep, cooking, consumption, clearing and dish washing)

THIS COUPON ENTITLES YOU TO

WET **PATCH AVOIDANCE**

Post coital pass to sleep on the dry side of the bed

I want to get

HOT & HEAVY

with you

I want to get

HOT & HEAVY

with you

THIS COUPON ENTITLES YOU TO

WATCH **BUT DON'T TOUCH**

Watch as I pleasure myself until climax. You can pleasure yourself as you watch
(no touching each other during the act. Post masturbation sex is permitted)

THIS COUPON ENTITLES YOU TO

SEX **SHOP**

Visit to the naughty shop! I'll let you pick an outfit or toy we can enjoy later

I want to get

HOT & HEAVY

with you

I want to get

HOT & HEAVY

with you

ONE **BONDAGE SESSION**

Someone is gong to be tied-up and f**ked tonight - you choose who
(the safe word is: _____)

ANAL **PLEASURE**

I'll let you play with my ass-hole. A finger, a tongue, a toy or something more

I want to get

HOT & HEAVY

with you

I want to get

HOT & HEAVY

with you

THIS COUPON ENTITLES YOU TO

PHONE **SEX SMUT**

I'll tell you all the dirty, smutty things I desperately want to do to you
(must not be in the same house or building at time of call)

THIS COUPON ENTITLES YOU TO

NO **PANTIES**

I'll go commando for the entire day
(spice things up further by combining with the Phone Sex coupon)

I want to get

HOT & HEAVY

with you

I want to get

HOT & HEAVY

with you

THIS COUPON ENTITLES YOU TO

A SEXY **GAMES NIGHT**

Think strip poker, naked Twister, dirty darts or something else

THIS COUPON ENTITLES YOU TO

STEAMY **SHOWER SEX**

Let's do it just like they do in the movies

I want to get

HOT & HEAVY

with you

I want to get

HOT & HEAVY

with you

THIS COUPON ENTITLES YOU TO

SEX **IN THE WILD**

Let's do it in the backyard, up against a tree, a secluded beach or elsewhere
(Disclaimer: keep it legal - any action you take is at your own risk)

THIS COUPON ENTITLES YOU TO

SENSUAL **LOVEMAKING**

Take it sloooow. Lots of touching, caressing, licking, panting and eye gazing

I want to get

HOT & HEAVY

with you

I want to get

HOT & HEAVY

with you

DISCOVERY **SEX**

Share three sexy things you enjoy or would like to try, then we'll do them

SEX **IN A TINY PLACE**

Like in the car, the closet or toilet

I want to get

HOT & HEAVY

with you

I want to get

HOT & HEAVY

with you

EROTIC **STORY TIME**

Up to 60 minutes (if we can last that long) of reading erotica to each other

ONE **INTIMACY WORKSHOP**

A tantric sex session, naked yoga, couples massage or something else

I want to get

HOT & HEAVY

with you

I want to get

HOT & HEAVY

with you

THIS COUPON ENTITLES YOU TO

PLAY **WITH ME ANYWAY**

Rub my throbbing penis while in a public place like an elevator or restaurant
(Be discreet, don't get caught - any action you take is at your own risk)

THIS COUPON ENTITLES YOU TO

CUDDLE & **KISSES**

Sometimes you just want to be held, adored and loved on
without taking it any further - here you go

I want to get

HOT & HEAVY

with you

I want to get

HOT & HEAVY

with you

WILDCARD COUPON

_____

WILDCARD COUPON

_____

I want to get

HOT & HEAVY

with you

I want to get

HOT & HEAVY

with you

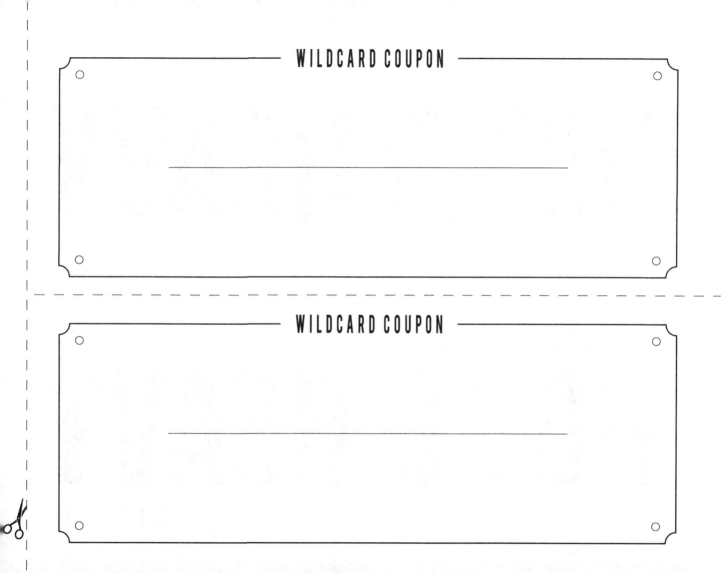

WILDCARD COUPON

WILDCARD COUPON

I want to get

HOT & HEAVY

with you

I want to get

HOT & HEAVY

with you

WILDCARD COUPON

_____

WILDCARD COUPON

_____

I want to get
HOT & HEAVY
with you

I want to get
HOT & HEAVY
with you

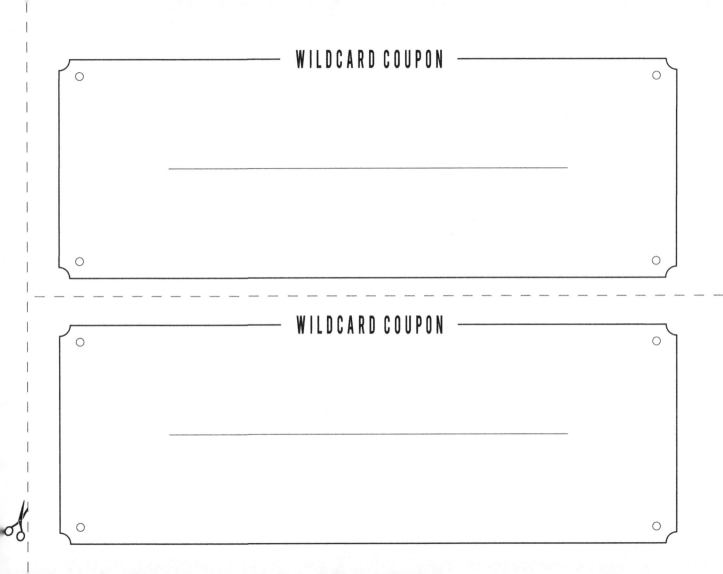

WILDCARD COUPON

WILDCARD COUPON

Made in the USA
Las Vegas, NV
16 January 2024